31 Diamond Thoughts

Vol. 1

Purpose & Relationships
Navigating Life With a Sense
of Contentment

Sharlene-Monique

Sunesis Ministries Ltd

Published by Sunesis Ministries Ltd. For more information about Sunesis Ministries Ltd, please visit:

www.stuartpattico.com

ISBN: 978-1-9163874-3-0

Contents

Foreword

I have had the honour of knowing Sharlene-Monique since she was a child and had the joy of watching her pursue her goals and dreams with great intention and tenacity. The words you will read in this, her debut offering, are exactly how she has lived her life: embracing the lessons of every circumstance and happening that comes her way, and living out the lessons with courage and in a way that teaches those of us looking on. I have long said that Sharlene is one of the healthiest people I know, and if you're reading this power-packed book, you will know why.

Whilst making being a wife, a mother, a daughter, a friend (I could go on) look easy, and slaying all day whilst doing so, she is quick to let us know that this is far from the truth, but that it can be done and done well. Honest, direct and plainly written, what Sharlene manages to do is give us all hope. She lets us know that we can do it, whilst making it clear that she herself is still on her journey. Isn't this the exciting stuff of life - the continuing and unfolding story being told, the dream yet to be fully realised?

I hope you enjoy these gems as much as I have. Sharlene's Diamond Thoughts are a personal invitation, with which she reaches her hand out to us, encouraging us to join her in the great adventure of life with bravery and hopeful expectation. I think I'll join her. You coming?

Karen Gibson MBE
Founder and Conductor of The Kingdom Choir

Acknowledgments

Thank you, my beautiful husband, for always being honest, giving unfiltered criticism and always supporting me. You and Tahlia are my world and, I love you both so much and the life we are building together. Thank you Mummy and Daddy for encouraging me to always go after the things I desire and pursue my dreams. Big Sis, I could never repay you for the time you invested into helping me make this book a reality. The bond and love are real. I am so blessed to have a big sister like you.

God, thank you for placing purpose and a thousand dreams inside of me. This book is the fruit of one of them and I'm looking forward to more.

What is a diamond woman?

'A Woman who is on her own journey and aligning with who she is meant to be, despite the outside noise and setbacks along the way. A Diamond will always be a diamond, even if she shines less on some days and on others is all brilliance'

Katriya Ross
'Writer and poet'

If you're reading this, I firstly want to say a big massive thank you for purchasing my first book. I'm excited about you going on this journey of exploration and guess what, it's exploring yourself. I know it might sound cliché, but as the saying goes, *Life is such a journey* and I really believe those words to be true. I feel like I'm growing constantly and that excites me, because the truth is, we're always changing, evolving and for me, that looks like having honest conversations with myself. These conversations help me discover what my fears are, what thought patterns I have chosen to believe and how can I grow in my character and become a better person. It can all feel a little intense to be honest, but it's not, because it doesn't all happen at once. It takes time and that's the fun part - there's no huge rush, so take the pressure off yourself and try to enjoy it.

In case you didn't know it already, 'You Are GREAT' and you have so much to offer your world. Sometimes we can't see our own greatness the way we should and we need to do a little work on ourselves. This journey will include some inspirational tips, random thoughts that have helped me along the way. Some of them are short and snappy and some are longer and more in-depth. I'll also be sharing my faith, some of my personal stories and life experiences that have helped to shape the person I'm becoming.

I'm not a counsellor, psychiatrist, or a relationship guru and I don't profess to have all the answers. I am simply someone who absolutely loves to encourage people and I truly believe we can all live a life filled with more joy than sadness. Even though we know we'll have good and bad times, it's just part of life; I'm really intentional about living my best life and feeling great in my mind, body and soul while I'm doing it. I hope this will be an enjoyable experience for you.

Big Love
Sharlene-Monique

'I am a woman I am a Diamond woman, I fill the world with my light'
Song: Diamond woman
EP: Perspective

1

Set high expectations for yourself

Set high expectations for yourself

I feel this is a great place for us to start this journey. This is a simple, gentle reminder for you to stay positive in your mind, because where the mind goes, the heart follows.

I have learnt over the years that what I expect is usually what will happen. Very often, because we feel like we have been disappointed by things in the past, it seems like nothing good will happen. This is a lie and it's not a good idea for you to entertain thoughts like that.

Good Things Will Happen' in your family, at work and in your personal life, but you have to believe that and speak it. In the same way, you may have convinced yourself that bad will happen, so change those thoughts to expect that good will happen. How do you do that? Focus only on the positive things in your life and do your best to have a high expectation for the future. The words that come out of your mouth are so important because you're a powerful person and your words will **CREATE YOUR WORLD**.

If this is something you don't do very often, then it might be a challenge at first, but try it and I guarantee you will reap the benefits. This book is a great place to start - expect this to be a good opportunity for you to assess some things about your life and yourself. It all starts in your mind and flows to your mouth, which will impact your actions. So be very selective about what you fill your mind with.

'Stop for a minute, breathe for a minute, it's not always how it seems, when you're chasing your dreams'
Song: Destiny
Destiny EP

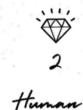

2

Human

Human

I was on my way to a rehearsal in Clapham Junction when a homeless man sitting on the road side caught my eye. It was a cold and wet winter's day, so I asked if I could purchase a meal and a hot drink for him. He responded by saying, 'I don't want anything from you. I have been sitting here for two days and no one has spoken to me; all I want is to have a conversation.' I was deeply moved by his response and immediately crouched down to engage with him. We spoke for around fifteen minutes and even though I don't remember what we spoke about, I do remember how thankful he was at the end of our chat. Conversing with the people around me is something I am privileged to be able to do on a daily basis, but it's easy to take these things for granted.

My dad runs a homeless charity whereby he provides breakfast once a month to the homeless community in Charing Cross. I have helped on a number of occasions and I remember speaking to one particular gentlemen. He told me that he was a qualified GP and used to have his own practice. Around ten years prior, his wife left him, along with his children. This led to him having a nervous breakdown. He ended up losing his house, his job and eventually became homeless. I was saddened to hear his story, but also honoured that he felt comfortable to share it with me.

As humans we are all so different, but also exactly the same. We all need each other; we can act like we don't need anyone but if we're honest, it's not true. Everyone needs someone and I believe we were created to navigate through life with love and connection. The two stories above, are a perfect example of this. You could be the richest person in the world, but your enjoyment of your riches would be limited if you don't have someone to lovingly share in it. These stories also reveal that hard times can come to anyone and it's so important to speak up and ask for help if you feel your mental health is being challenged. I wonder if that man who lost his family and job spoke out before things got too heavy. Very often there is a chain of events that lead to a situation like that.

If you see that someone around you is struggling, take the time to check in on them, especially those who always seem the strongest. Very often, they are the ones who most need someone to ask if they are okay. Remember, that there is so much more that unites us than divides us and when it's all said and done, we all bleed the same and we all need love and connection. We are all human!

'We all need love and hope in this thing we call life'
Song: Human
Perspective EP

3

You don't ask you don't get

You don't ask you don't get

Around five years ago I had an administration job. I was a very committed worker and I know the managers were happy with my work because they would request that I train all the new members of staff from different locations. After working there for approximately two and a half years I began to wonder why a pay rise had not been mentioned and it bothered me. I spoke to my dad about it, offloading my frustration and he asked me one simple question, 'Have you asked them if you can have one?' I responded (again with an attitude), 'Why should I have to ask? In all my other jobs the manager has done a yearly appraisal. I have been assessed and then my pay was increased.' My dad simply responded with, *'You don't ask, you don't get!'* and walked off.

When I really sat and pondered about it, I was a little scared to ask, because I thought they might see it as cheeky. Nonetheless, I got over myself and plucked up the courage to ask one of my company directors. I began by explaining how much work I did. I explained the value I brought to the company and that I felt this should be rewarded. Before I could even finish my speech, he stopped me and said, 'You're absolutely right and I would be happy to give you one. Contact your line manager and explain the situation and we'll get that sorted right away.' I was so shocked for two reasons. I couldn't believe the meeting had gone so well and because he agreed with everything I had said. Before I left, I asked, 'Why hasn't this happened before and will my co-worker receive a pay rise as well?' My manager's response was, 'You never asked for one before and neither has the other staff, so I would appreciate it if this stayed confidential.'

I'm sure you can see exactly where I'm going with this. I learnt a few lessons from this experience, the main one being - sometimes life is not fair! I did feel badly for the others. There are so many things we can get from life if we ask, because what's the worst that can happen? In this case, my manager could have said no, but I wouldn't have lost anything and I had so much to gain. Make sure you take every opportunity with both hands and ask the questions that can lead you to potential treasures.

4

Nope, there's no traffic

Nope, there's no traffic

Growing up, I would hear my dad say *'Know who you are and be who you are*!' I'm really thankful for both of my parents and the impact they've had on my life. My dad always had these one-liners that have stuck with me.

It's become really popular to speak about being 'good enough' and to 'love who you are', that sometimes these words don't sink in the way they're meant to. When I realised and I mean, really realised that out of the seven billion plus people living on the planet there really was no one like me, it changed everything. My faith and belief systems have really helped me to realise that I don't need to compete or compare with anyone because even though there are so many singers in the industry, they can't be me, I can't be them and that is where I find my POWER! The author Bill Johnson says, *'If you knew who God made you to be, you'd never want to be anyone else.'* I believe these words completely, not to only sound confident, I actually do believe every word and it has impacted every area of my life.

I want people to like me, but if they don't, I'm honestly not fussed. I really believe the people I have around me are meant to be there and I take my friendship circle very seriously. I'm not defined by being liked because I know I add value. It's such a great feeling to know you have something to offer, but your goal is not to be the best, rather, to be the best version of yourself. You were created to bring something unique to the planet and I know it's unique because no two people can do any activity exactly the same way. Be great and occupy your lane with confidence, knowing that you are the best at being you.

'Oh, oh there's no one like you, there's no one like you'
Song: You
Destiny EP

5

No one is perfect – that's okay

No one is perfect – that's okay

We never want to feel like we've stopped growing, because we are ever changing people. Life changes us, circumstances impact us for better or for worse. You and I are going to make mistakes, say the wrong things and at times do the wrong thing. What really matters is how you allow these moments to help you grow. Learn to be open to the people who know and care about you and who you trust to challenge you. Mistakes happen, so pause, reflect, apologise, forgive yourself and move on. Sometimes fixing it means apologising, at other times it means making sacrifices to make things right that could cause you to feel exposed or embarrassed. That's okay, because when you have tried, you'll sleep better knowing you invested a lot of effort into getting the right result.

Mistakes are your stepping stones of growth for a greater tomorrow.

6

Be kind to you

Be kind to you

Rewind the clock about fourteen years and I would never have taken a photo which showed my legs. It wasn't because I didn't like taking pictures, or wearing nice pretty clothes, you see, sharing pictures with my legs showing is quite a big deal for me. It's proof of where I have reached in the journey towards loving myself. Fourteen years ago, I would have never worn anything revealing my pins, because I really used to hate my legs. Summer was a sad time for me because I lived in jeans and leggings.

I was born with a birth mark on my left calf, and as I got older it grew with me, leaving a rather large, light mark on my leg. I have other scars and blemishes on my legs too, and because of this, decided my legs were not worthy of being shown to the world. At one point it got so bad that I wanted to go to a laser surgeon. Hatred of my legs literally consumed my thoughts day and night... but not anymore. To some, this might seem boastful, but I absolutely love my legs now and they look pretty much the same as they did fourteen years ago.

For me, the turning point happened when my sister, Natalie, forced me to put on a pair of shorts and look at myself in the mirror. I really didn't want to, as I had done this before and it usually resulted in tears, but I did it. She began to tell me that I looked gorgeous, but I didn't believe her. In an effort to convince me, she called her fiancé (at the time) and asked him if he saw anything wrong with my legs and he said they seemed perfectly fine. I can remember being shocked as he shared what men look for: 'no hairs' and 'soft legs'. I'm not sure if it was because he was a man (and has always been like a big brother to me), but I started to think that maybe he was right. The very next day I decided to wear a pair of shorts and fight the negative thoughts in my mind. I also started to tell myself that I was beautiful, every day, and I prayed for God to help me to truly love who I was, and He did! One of the greatest things you can do to improve your self-confidence is to start celebrating yourself every day, and trust me, you will start to believe you are beautiful. It feels amazing to be free from all the lies in my mind.

Self-acceptance is a journey, and the confidence you see on my social media pages was not something I gained overnight, but I am living proof that it is possible. There is no magic remedy, you start by making the decision to love all of who you are and accepting yourself every single day. I know it might sound simple, but do that for three-hundred and sixty-five days and it's highly likely that your attitude will change dramatically. Very often we want a quick fix and an overnight transformation, but that's not realistic. Focus on making this new way of thinking a lifestyle and not a quick exercise. A great man named Christian Tapper said 'To be a woman is to be beautiful'. You are a masterpiece.

'You're beautiful just the way you are, no one's perfect but you're not far off'
Song: YOU
Destiny EP

7

Enjoyment

Enjoyment

When I look back over my life from childhood into my adult years, there were and still are so many 'Normal Days'. You know what I mean, you're doing the same things from day-to-day, like going to school, working at the same job you've been in for years, doing the school run, cooking dinner every night and life can feel like you are on a hamster wheel. Eighty per cent of life (in my opinion) looks and feels just like this and twenty per cent will include lovely days out, fun adventures, beautiful holidays etc. For some of us, we dread that eighty per cent and we struggle to find joy in it. What If I told you that you have the ability to enjoy every day of your life simply by having the correct perspective?

A few years back, I worked in a primary school with five hundred children. It was four days a week and I lived for my long weekend, because I didn't work on Fridays. I taught the entire school music lessons, led two to three assemblies each week. In addition, I spent many hours preparing lesson plans with pictures and videos on my power point presentation, in an effort to try and engage the children and get them to love music. I feel badly saying this, but for a good while I hated it! It wasn't the children. They were lovely and I know they enjoyed me being their teacher, because they would tell me. However, when your dream since you were five years old is to be a singer, it's a struggle to find joy doing something you feel you weren't made for, no matter how good you are at it.

I can remember one particular day feeling so down about the job and I randomly heard God say (in my mind), 'Find the Awe and Wonder'. I began to ponder on this and realised that even though I found the job quite challenging, I had the opportunity to make a huge impact in these little peoples' lives. I remember the teachers at my school when I was growing up, who really cared and I also remember the ones who didn't. I realised that I could say something to these children or teach a song that could potentially stay with them forever and from that moment on, I found so much fulfilment and joy in the job. Unfortunately, when I was leaving, the head teacher did not allow me to say goodbye to the children. This was really hard for me to deal with. Around a year after I left, I received a private message from their new music teacher on Instagram and she said *'Hey Sharlene, I just wanted to send a message because I've heard so much about you. I've been teaching music at your old school for 5 months now and the teachers and kids always talk about how awesome you were'.* This was the exact message I needed, of reassurance, that I made an impact in that school and I did it with JOY!

Joy is always a choice; your perspective can change everything. You only have one life, make sure you enjoy it with intention.

'Always, never I'll forget to look outside the box and love the little things always'
Song: Awe And Wonder
Destiny EP

8

Do what works for you

Do what works for you

My husband and I always wanted children. It was something we spoke about in length whilst dating. When we got married, we randomly said we would wait two years before starting a family, but deep down we both knew we were open to waiting longer. For some strange reason, a few people seemed to have an opinion on when we should have children. We received comments like, 'Don't wait too long', 'Trust me if it's money you'll be fine'. I actually had someone try to make me feel badly by saying how glad they were that they had all their children before thirty as she wanted to be a young mum and not an old mum like me (I was thirty years old). I know – shocking, right? I've always been amazed at how people try to put their own insecurities or fears onto others, but that's a whole other diamond thought. Since the age of twenty-three, I fell in love with fitness, working out and eating healthily, so feeling old and having no energy for children was never a fear of mine.

I was never really a 'Kids Person' growing up - you know, those people who adore all children and have to hold all the babies they come into contact with - that's my husband. I can't lie, that's not me and it never has been. I like to enjoy the children I have a connection with. It wasn't that I didn't feel maternal, because when my sister had her two children, she had to keep reminding me that she had given birth to them, as I was behaving as if I was convinced that they were mine. Deep down I wanted to feel ready for the sacrifice I knew would be required when I eventually had them. If I'm going to be really honest, I was enjoying building my career, travelling, working abroad, working with Chris and quite simply, having an absolutely care free life.

After being married for six years, whilst on tour in America at a hotel in West Port Connecticut, I could no longer pretend that the symptoms I was feeling were in my head. The pregnancy test was positive and we were indeed one hundred per cent pregnant. I jumped and danced all around that hotel room, because by this time I really wanted a baby. Deep down, I always knew that I would feel this way when the time was right for me. It just so happened that my husband felt the same way and it felt like the perfect time for us and our journey.

Someone is always going to have something to say about what you do, but you're the only person who has to live with your decisions. Please don't take what I'm saying out of context, because I think it's important to have people around who you trust and who challenge you, but when it comes down to it, always make sure you do what works for you, because you're the only one who has to live with your decisions.

*'Let me breathe, let me be outside your inequality, I'm a butterfly
flying free'
Song: Diamond Woman
Perspective EP*

9

Boundaries are a good thing

Boundaries are a good thing

Boundaries: *'A line which marks the limits of an area; a dividing line'*[1].

In my opinion, the subject of boundaries comes in two parts, learning when to say 'Yes' and when to say 'No'. Not everyone in your life should have the same access to you; you should have different spaces for different people, work colleagues, friends and family.

Family comes first. My husband and daughter are my number one priority, along with my immediate family. Family isn't always who you have a blood connection with. I also have friends who are more like blood relatives. If my family need me, I'm there without hesitation. That level of support has been modelled to me by my parents and sister throughout my whole life. There really is not much I wouldn't tell them and little to nothing I wouldn't do for them if they needed me. They mean the world to me.

---

[1] https://www.lexico.com/definition/boundary accessed 7th October 2021

The friends I hold dearly will always get a lot of my time and attention. I have friends who are mentors, who support and encourage me. These people are priceless to me as they have wisdom and experience that I don't have. I also have people younger than me who I mentor and they have a certain level of access to me because it's important that I give as well as receive. Then there are my friends who I do life with and even though I encourage them, they also encourage me. Again, within these friendships there is trust and I will share personal information and experiences with them, but I do still have boundaries. There are things about my marriage, family and personal goals that I wouldn't share with my friends. I obviously can't list what should and shouldn't be shared as it's a personal thing, but for example, some of the conversations my husband and I have are private and no one else should be privy to them.

Lastly, we have acquaintances: *'A person one knows slightly, but who is not a close friend'*[2].

---

[2] https://www.lexico.com/definition/acquaintance accessed 7th October 2021

Unfortunately, this is where things can sometimes get blurry.

These people within my life have little to no personal access to me, but sometimes people place a higher value on you than you do on them, it's just a harsh reality of life. I'm a very friendly person and if I can help someone, I will. However, sometimes people can over-step the boundaries in this area. I don't take the word 'friendship' lightly. A light-hearted conversation where we might connect on a subject doesn't make us friends, in my opinion. Do not confuse connection and relationship with environment and common ground conversation. A work colleague I spend an hour at lunch with due to being in the same environment is an acquaintance, not a friend.

I'm learning more and more that that's okay.

I am extremely private and even though I love to share my experiences, there is so much I don't share and I like it that way. I don't think there is anything wrong with that and I can't apologise for the way I feel. Keep your boundaries clear, love people, be polite and don't be afraid to be firm if you need to protect your peace.

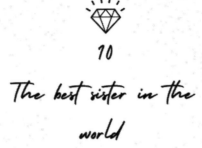

10

The best sister in the world

The best sister in the world

Like most siblings, my sister Natalie and I used to fight when we were little. She's older than me by two years and eight months and there were a good few years when we were younger, that I annoyed her, because she was maturing and I was still in that younger stage of life.

I used to be so jealous of her because I didn't feel great about myself growing up and I struggled with my self-esteem. She has always shone and was great at every and any sport she tried, really pretty, confident and had a four pack since she was twelve or thirteen. Before my parents moved house when I was fourteen, we really clashed, primarily because we needed our own space and at the time, we had to share a room. Once we moved house and I grew up a little, we became besties. My dad also has a lot to do with our bond because if he heard us fighting, he wouldn't allow it and he'd say, 'You two will be close, you are all each other have, so stop the noise.' At the time it was so frustrating, but now those words have become our reality.

My sister hasn't changed much over the years, and one thing that has remained constant and consistent is her overwhelming love and care for me. She has always looked out for me, done her best to encourage me and taught me about fashion and femininity. To be honest, I've watched her do this for all her close friends over the years because she is what you would call a 'Giver' and an 'Empath'. If she considers you a close friend, then she sees you as family and her love is big, very wide and extremely generous. I'm honestly not saying any of this to sound nice; she is such a special person and it's hard to imagine my life without her in it. She's a master hair stylist by profession but what she does for her clients is so much more than just a hair style, she encourages every person who sits in her chair. Everything she does is done with excellence from her work ethic, to her marriage and raising her two children. The problem with being this wonderful is that sometimes people take advantage of you and sometimes you give so much that there isn't much left for you.

There have been moments where she's been hurting on the inside, but because everything looks so perfect on the outside, people don't really see her. I'm embarrassed to say that I have taken advantage of her kind nature before and I'm not proud of that, but now I truly do see her and it's my goal to support, love and be there for her as much as I can be. If you're anything like her or know anyone like her, you'll know these individuals are like very special treasure. Over the years, I've watched her take her power back and put herself and her health first and she's flourished because of that. For those reading this, maybe I'm describing your partner, mum, dad, brother or an uncle or grandparent. Whoever that person is, take the time to really see them, because even though they love to give and they care so deeply, they also need to receive and be shown just as much love.

Make sure you take the time to truly see the special people in your life and don't take them for granted. If you haven't told them in a while, maybe today's the day to let them know how important they are to you. Your words could be the exact thing they need to lift their spirit.

11

Marriage is....

Marriage is....

.....not about cute photos, glamorous weddings, pretty children and looking like you have the perfect relationship. Marriage is a constant act of SELF DENIAL, accepting the other's imperfections, loving each other through personal challenges, not being right all the time and learning how to practice INSTANT FORGIVENESS.

Marriage is about having hard conversations and working through arguments that will leave you extremely emotional and cause you to question whether the person you have chosen was the right choice. It's about money and finances, creating legacy and making constant sacrifices, because that is what's best for your relationship.

Lastly, it's about learning to hear and not just listen (this has been major for me). It is being respectful at all times whilst challenging each other to continue to grow, when you see character traits that need to be worked on. It's about humility and choosing to love daily when you don't feel like being loving! ALWAYS listening to God and allowing Him to lead, because He created both of you and knows what you both need more than you do.

Marriage is beautiful and fun, but the things listed above are also some of the realities of marriage and seldom do I hear them spoken of. I am learning to embrace every aspect of our journey...

'Through thick and thin they chose to win, love found a way'
Song: Stay
Perspective EP

12

Intention

Intention

'When someone shows you who they are believe them'
Maya Angelou

A friend of mine asked me for advice regarding her boyfriend. She said they had been dating for around a year and she hoped it was leading to marriage but she couldn't figure out what his intentions were because of some of the things he would say and do. He never invited her to spend time with his family and friends and when she tried to have vulnerable conversations about money or planning for the future, he would get defensive and shut the conversation down. I asked my husband, Chris, what his thoughts were and he simply said, *'When a man wants to be with you he makes it clear'*.

The word that comes to mind is 'intention' - *'A mental state that represents a commitment to carrying out an action or actions in the future.'* Her boyfriend's intentions were not clear which left her with some decisions to make. She told me that before her current partner, she had been single for ten years, she felt worried about the prospect of leaving him and being alone. That relationship did eventually end because it was better for her to be single than to stay with someone who didn't value her the way she deserved. She later got married to a very spectacular man who respects and loves her.

Yes, I am married, but before my wedding I enjoyed my single life and spent no time on men who were not deserving of me. You must know your worth, because if you don't value and love yourself first, it will be hard for you to receive that love from anyone else. To the beautiful lady reading this who is dating someone whose intentions do not match your values and your desire to get married, do not let fear make you settle for someone who is not right for you. It might be scary and daunting, but every day with the wrong person is one less day spent embracing the precious moments of your life, learning and evolving, whether in a relationship or not. A lot of emphasis is placed around relationships but learn to appreciate being single, because that's when you grow and with that growth you come to know what you're looking for. Do not allow your singleness to become your identity, because being a happy, wholesome human is the goal with or without a partner.

'Evolving daily living my best life, this space I'm in, there's no compromise'
Song: Diamond Woman
Perspective EP

13

Big things start small

Big things start small

'You don't have to be great to get started but you do need to get started to be great'
Zig Ziglar

Sometimes we limit our capabilities because we think we need to have everything perfect all at once. The truth is, 'Big Things Start Small' and you must not despise the day of small beginnings. Every success story has a beginning and for most people, it's not a glamorous one.

I started singing in church around four years old to audiences that were no bigger than approximately one-hundred people or less. I've always loved singing and performing and for as long as I can remember, I've loved the stage. It came very naturally to me and I always felt at home there. I would imagine myself singing in front of thousands of people. I didn't know how or when that would happen but I saw it in my mind. Who knew that in 2018 I would be part of the Kingdom Choir and sing in front of two BILLION households? Karen, our choir director, says it was an 'undreamt dream' and I think I agree.

Start small. Be consistent. Have integrity and see value in the seemingly insignificant moments when no one is watching. Integrity is one of my absolute core values and I believe that it also adds to your self-esteem. Every time you say you're going to do something and you do it, you're respecting yourself and the people around you. This does not go unnoticed.

I could list a number of celebrities who have had a similar experience. Steve Harvey quit his job, ended up homeless and was booed off the stage in the early days of his stand-up career. Now he has his own radio, TV and games show. JK Rowling was on benefits, struggling to pay her rent, before she was discovered and now, she is one of the world's best-selling authors. Oprah was told she wasn't right for TV and now owns her own television station. I'll say it again, 'Big Things Start Small', so get started! Take a step of faith and go for it. There is absolutely no failure, just lots of opportunities to grow.

'What you see isn't where you are; the destination isn't very far'
Song: Destiny
Destiny EP

14

You can't feel bad
about the truth: wrong
is wrong

You can't feel bad about the truth: wrong is wrong

Gossip: 'Casual or unconstrained conversation or reports about other people, typically involving details which are not confirmed as true'[3].

I've never been interested in gossip, he said she said conversations do not edify me. But there is a difference between gossip and sharing your truth. A few years back, I was speaking with one of my close friends and we share a mutual friend who had said a number of questionable things to me. You know, those comments that demonstrate the person may have an issue with them-self, but they act like you are the issue. I felt so badly about vocalising it, because it seemed wrong to externally process it with another person. This is because I don't think it's okay to be hurt by someone and then tell anyone and everyone who will listen about what they've done, as it would ruin their reputation.

If you discuss or process something with a friend who is trust-worthy and has a willing ear to listen and not repeat the conversation so that healing can take place, then it's

---

[3] https://www.lexico.com/definition/gossip accessed 7th October 2021

okay. Once I spoke about it and got feedback, my friend explained that 'You can't feel bad about sharing your truth.' If someone hurts you, it serves no one to hold it in and act like nothing happened, because that just causes more pain. When you're open and honest, you can then decide if you want to confront that person or create some boundaries to protect yourself, moving forward. One of my biggest tools when someone hurts me is prayer. I pray about anything and everything and God speaks to me either directly, through the Bible, through music, or through family and friends (more about that in thought no 30). Sometimes I'll realise that maybe the issue is me, or I'll try to see what the person who hurt me might be going through to cause them to hurt me. I have learnt that 'hurt people, hurt people'. This always helps me to not take offence and I can usually brush things off easily by processing internally. Of course, this does not excuse their actions, but it means that I'll feel no need to avoid them when I see them next and I can still show them love.

It's not easy to show love to people who hurt us, but that's why forgiveness is not about the other person, it's actually about you. Please don't misread what I'm saying - there are times when people show us who they are and we have to make a decision to either keep them in our lives or not, after all, you are not a door mat. But there are also times when people hurt us and they have no idea of the pain they've caused. If that person means something to you, it's important for you to tell them rather than act like everything is okay. Healthy confrontation is a great thing and there doesn't need to be any shouting or screaming, it can look like a calm conversation where both parties express their truth. If the relationship is meant to continue it will and your bond will hopefully be stronger because of it. But it's not your role to manage how they deal with your truth even if they didn't mean to cause you pain. Keeping things bottled inside is so bad for our mental and spiritual health.

Looking after you involves being selective about who you have in your space and as much as this is a hard truth to take, not everyone is for you - fact. Some people unfortunately, because of where they are at, can't be happy for you when you are excelling and they project their issues onto you. Sometimes the only option is to stay away from those individuals, put your well-being first and most importantly keep speaking your truth.

'Someone's journey is different to mine, life experience has
taught me well.
I know we all have an opportunity to grow'
Song: Human
Perspective EP

15

It's okay to not be okay

It's okay to not be okay

It's Thursday 16th April 2020 at 1.16 in the morning and exactly two weeks since I lost my beautiful Aunty Heather and the coolest uncle in the world, my lovely Uncle Selvin within a day of each other.

It's currently lock down season and I'm six months pregnant. Today is what I would have called a good day, as I woke up without that that deep sense of sadness I have felt ever since they passed. I've just finished playing voice notes on WhatsApp from my aunty and watching a lovely video (I must have watched it around fifty times by now) of my uncle and I'm an absolute bawling mess. I was doing so well today. I prayed, did some work which has been a myth lately and spent three plus hours outside in the garden getting some very much needed vitamin D, whilst enjoying the chirpy birds around me.

Despite all my efforts to try and hold it all together and manage my emotions, that deep sad feeling found its way back this evening and I have to once again accept that I'm not okay. I pride myself on being a really happy, joyous person. It's not something I pretend to be, it's just who I am. I'm very intentional about what I read, what I feed my mind with and I keep thankfulness as my focus; it always makes me feel better. Here I am, pregnant with my first child kicking away in my belly and even though I thank God every day for her, I have to admit that I'm not okay and I am learning, that is okay!

Life can throw us some real challenges. For me, right now it's grief and the loss of two people who meant more to me than I could even begin to try and articulate. Sometimes when really hard things happen, we want to fix them, solve them and make them better really quickly, I know I do! But for the first time in my life, none of my tricks are working and I have decided that I am okay with that. I'm not sure when I will feel differently, but I do know that as each day goes by, even though it hasn't got easier, I adjust a tiny bit more than I did the day before, to the reality of them being gone. So, today if you're going through something similar, I want you to know you have permission to feel everything you're feeling. If like me, your emotions are like the biggest roller coaster and the smallest trigger makes you burst into tears, it's okay to NOT be okay!

*'I have so many questions, so many things that I want to know,
like why did this thing happen'*
Song: Life
Perspective EP

16

Stop sprinting and begin to jog

Stop sprinting and begin to jog

I'm not sure if I was born this way, or if it happened whilst growing up, but I evolved into a rather impatient person. I look back sometimes and can see where this wasn't necessarily my best attribute, however, my impatience and problem-solving attitude ensured I always got things done. I would want things to happen immediately, wanting my plans to materialise right away, without having to wait. I'm also the kind of person who's willing to put in the ten thousand hours to make it happen, but very often things don't work that way.

Process − *'A series of actions or steps taken in order to achieve a particular end'*[4]. We can't skip the steps in our journey to get to the desired end and in many cases, there is no end. When your goal is to become a better person, you grow in character. I am convinced that this is a constant on-going journey of growth that has no destination. Some achievements have a finish line; however, I believe that the journey to reach the goal is more important than the goal itself. We learn so much

---

[4] https://www.lexico.com/definition/process accessed 7th October 2021

when things don't go the way we plan, such as patience. Sometimes we just need to take a leisurely jog, maybe even a walk and stop sprinting ahead, because in my opinion, you'll only delay the journey more from burning out, or causing damage to a limb by trying to do something you're not quite ready for. In addition, the quality of what you want to achieve won't be there.

Always focus on quality, not quantity. Be patient with YOUR process and remember you're an individual; your steps look different to others. Lastly, try your best to enjoy your current view as you move closer to your goal.

'Frustration is gripping, time feels like it's slipping away from me,
I wanna give up but my heart wants to sing this sweet melody'
Song: Destiny
Destiny EP

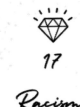

17

Racism

Racism

I was five years old the first time I experienced racism. I had popped out of class with my blonde hair, blue eyed friend to get some water from the fountain. She began to splash me and I joined in. My teacher heard the laughter, rushed out of class and began to shout, 'What are you two doing? Sally go back into class right now!' Then, with a completely different tone of voice, she continued, 'Sharlene, go and sit in the corner with your hands on your head and DO NOT MOVE until I tell you to.' I couldn't understand why I was being punished and my friend wasn't. At the time I didn't know this was called racism, I just knew it did not feel right. There were a number of other issues I won't go into with this said teacher, but let's just say that I'm so glad my dad is who he is because when he found out, he went straight to the head teacher to complain.

Unfortunately, it didn't stop there. Fast forward approximately sixteen years later to when I worked for a certain bank, where I could do nothing right in the eyes of my white manager. My colleague (again blue eyed with blonde hair) knew I wanted a particular day off that she also wanted, so she expressed that it was fair that I ask our manager first. I requested the day and was immediately denied it because apparently, she didn't have enough staff on that day. My colleague who did the exact same job as me asked for the same date and was given the time off. It's subtle and could be seen by some as a coincidence, but it was blatant racism.

There are so many stereotypes around young black boys. When I look at my beautiful nephew, Josiah, I have to manage my emotions sometimes. To many, he would be seen as a trouble-maker just because he is black and if he had a hoodie on his head then more labels get added. But instead, I see a young eleven-year-old boy, a straight 'A' student who has always excelled academically. Loves football and is great at anything sports related. He's happy, loves food, is respectful and loves his family. The truth is, racism feels like a never-ending problem and even though I wish there was a clear-cut solution, I am reminded of the fact that, *'Small steps make big steps and big steps mean those steps were not in vain'* (Song: Human). We all have the opportunity to play our part.

1 Corinthians 13:13 (NKJV) - "...the greatest of these is love".

A few books to read for education:

- Why I'm No Longer Talking to White People About Race - Reni Eddo-Lodge
- Natives – Akala
- I Am Not Your Baby Mother – Candice Brathwaite
- Sister Sister – Candice Brathwaite

18

My skin is just

perfect

My skin is just perfect

I can remember being sixteen years old, I had just started college. It was an exciting time for me because I went to a girls' only secondary school. Of course, the ladies were checking out all the good-looking guys and vice-versa. On my fourth day, there was a list the boys had made to celebrate the girls they thought were the most attractive. A few of my friends had seen the list before me and said my name was on it. I definitely wanted to see what category they had placed me in.

'Girl with the nicest hairstyle – Sharlene Rodney', it said - so far, so good. 'Best-looking dark-skinned girl – Sharlene Rodney'! It was at that moment that my face dropped, because in my opinion I was not dark-skinned. I was offended that I had been placed in a category that I felt did not represent me. I can remember asking one of the boys why my name was there because, I reasoned, *'I am not dark-skinned'*. He responded by saying, *'You're not dark-skinned compared to who?'* I was stunned, and began to wonder why this had offended me. It's not until a few years ago whilst processing this with a friend, I realised that our concept of 'blackness' had been redefined; the bar of beauty had become the lightest of the light. It was clear that I had been seen as dark-skinned, because to him, there was no beauty in the dark-skinned woman; they had been rendered invisible.

I like that our children will see women such as Alex Wek and Lupita Nyong'o who have all been featured in major magazines such as *Vogue* and *Elle*. More recently, the stunning Khoudia Diop, also known as the Melanin Goddess, who has conquered the internet, completely shattered stereotypical beauty standards. But, it frustrates me that this would somehow make it all okay now, and I do question if this is some sort of tokenism. All shades and colours must be represented because they are all beautiful. We women must compliment and celebrate each other.

To any of my readers who have ever struggled with the complexion of your skin, I am here to tell you that you are so beautiful, stunning and gorgeous. Your skin is perfect whether you're dark chocolate, caramel, vanilla, olive or honey-skinned. You are a beautiful radiant queen and you must love all of who you are, despite the opinion of others.

'Why won't you just let your quirks shine on through, the best demonstration of yourself is being you'
Song: You
Destiny EP

19

Let's talk about pregnancy weight

Let's talk about pregnancy weight

Firstly, it's important that we normalise weight gain in pregnancy. It's not something to feel ashamed or embarrassed about. I went up two dress sizes, added six inches to my waist and I was one-hundred per cent OK with it. I was in awe at what my body had done and I refused to place pressure on myself and do crash diets. I spent so many years hating my body and now I really do love it. I make no apologies for that.

One year later in July 2021, I had lost five inches around my waist and I began to fit into my old skinny jeans. It felt good, but it was no walk in the park. Before I got pregnant, I was extremely fit and I had been naive in thinking that once my baby was born, I would be able to jump back into the prior consistent workout routine. At around six months, I attempted to do a two-week shred of intense workouts and I lasted four days. Tahlia was still waking up three to four times a night and I was exhausted from it all. Then came weaning and transitioning her from exclusively breastfeeding to bottle milk only. That was one of the most traumatising experiences for me and Tahlia since becoming a mother. She just would not take the bottle and because I had tried to stop in the daytime and give her the bottle at night which she refused, I decided I had to stop abruptly. On the first day of weaning, she cried all night, it was so hard to see her like that, but I had to be strong. Nine days later, I can confirm that I won the battle and she drank a bottle.

All of this contributed to how hard I could do workouts. Some weeks I would manage three workouts, at other times, one to two and during a really busy week, nothing. But I would do my best to eat healthy foods, which consisted of lots of greens, smoothies, fish and vegetables. I removed meat from my diet completely at around six months post-partum, for health reasons and this contributed to my overall health and my skin really improved. With all the new challenges and the allotted time I had to work out, due to caring for Tahlia, small consistent steps were what got me to my goal. I wish I could tell you that I took shortcuts, but I didn't. I'm a firm believer in implementing a healthy lifestyle, because if you do, it's unlikely that you'll put the weight back on. If I wanted a treat, I would give myself one, because when it comes to food, it's all about moderation and when I was having an exhausting day, Haagen Daz was my best friend.

When I look back at my pregnancy photos, my face didn't change much until around four weeks before Tahlia's birth. My nose looked swollen, my face was definitely very round and after I gave birth, even my eyes looked puffy because of water retention. I did not rush this weight loss journey, I took my sweet time and did what I could, when I could and made things work around Tahlia. Go easy on yourself and remember that you carried LIFE inside of you; it's a very BIG DEAL! I do all of this for me. It makes me feel amazing and happy and I am committed to being my best self. If you feel good with the extra weight, that's fine, but if you don't, take the pressure off and try to embrace your individual journey. It could take months or years before you are back to your pre-baby weight and there's nothing wrong with that. What if your body never returns to the size it was before? Would you be able to accept the change? When you become a mother, there are so many things you're dealing with, from hormones to complete exhaustion, so go easy on yourself. PERFECTION does not exist - do what works for you and be true to who you are.

'Black or golden hair it's lovely all the same, small or bigger
cheeks your smile radiates''
Song: You
Destiny EP

20

You can't change
people you can only

encourage

You can't change people you can only encourage

I absolutely love to see the people in my life win in whatever they are passionate about. It really does make me happy and if I can help in any way to achieve a goal, I'm all in. I would say I'm very goal driven - I say something, I plan and then execute. Sometimes I don't even know how I'm going to take the ideas I have in my head and make them a reality, but I just start somewhere and take it from there. I'm also someone who likes to keep growing whether that's in regard to the books I'm reading, health and fitness, my faith in God and character or personal goals. I like constructive criticism from the people close to me and mentors, because all these things help to challenge me and aid me in my growth. I never want to stop growing and learning.

If I love and care for you and I see an area that I feel could be developed, or I see a talent or gift that is not being used, it's like something comes over me and I want to make it my mission to help the people closest to me live a full life of purpose. I'm such an ambassador for living life to the full and loving it. That does not mean it's always going to be perfect, but whilst God gives me breath, I plan to try to enjoy every day as much as possible.

Even though this is something I'm passionate about, I have to be careful about not pushing the boundaries. It does not matter how much potential I see in those close to me or how much help I'm willing to give. Everyone has to live the life they choose and you can't change a person to fit your ideal; for them, all you can do is encourage them. I must be honest and say that I have struggled with this, especially with people I really love. Everyone has the right to live the life they choose. My job is to be there for them, as and when they need me. This can be a hard truth to accept (it has been for me), but once you accept it, you will feel lighter, knowing that even though you might not agree with the choices being made, you can still show love and give your support.

'Sometimes we feel like we need to do big things for everyone, often it's the little things that bring the biggest change'
Song: Human
Perspective EP

21

Mummy's cooking = happiness

Mummy's cooking = happiness

My mum is honestly, the best cook in the whole entire world. I know that many of you would say the same about your mum, given the chance, but TRUST ME, my mum can cook anything and is a master at Caribbean cuisine. Growing up, my dad was a minister in the church (he's a pastor now) but even without the title, he is the person who always looked for the new family at church and he would invite them for Sunday dinner. When I was a child, there were always people visiting to stay the night, to spend time with the family and most importantly eat mummy's food. At the time I didn't understand how important that was for the people who were invited, I just felt sorry for my sister who had to give up her big bedroom (and sleep in mine) and sometimes I didn't feel like talking and getting to know people, but now as an adult, I understand.

Sometimes my dad would tell my mum the day before, or even on the day, that someone, or a group were coming for dinner and she would get so stressed about it. Looking back now and understanding what it takes to host people and prepare, I can relate to some of her frustrations, but at the time I found it funny and strange. Funny, simply because sometimes kids laugh at their parents, but strange because once she had prepared the food, it was always amazing and I'm not just saying that. I can't remember one occasion where she burnt the food, or didn't prepare enough and the compliments she received afterwards always put the biggest smile on her face.

My mum's contribution to our family through her cooking is such a major part of our celebrations. Easter would not be the same without her fried snapper, with all the marinated onions and peppers, home-made coleslaw and a nice chunk of hard dough bread. Christmas wouldn't be the same without her duck, barbeque ribs, or her grilled chicken. All my mum's dishes are delicious, bringing so much joy to our family and to anyone who has the pleasure of experiencing it.

My mum and I are quite different. She does not love the stage, she's not a singer and our personalities are quite opposite in many ways. Even though she has taught me to cook and I can do it, I don't love it like she does, and that's okay. What she brings to the world is just as important as what I bring and it's really hard for me to imagine life without her funny comments, silly jokes, her love and of course her food. I'm sharing this because sometimes we don't realise the impact of what we bring to the people around us and what it does for those close to us. Maybe you're like my mum and you love to cook too. Whatever it is that you enjoy might be small to you or even easy, but it means a lot to the people around you who need you. You have so much value...

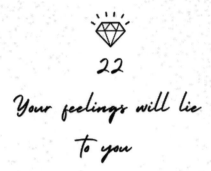

22

Your feelings will lie to you

Your feelings will lie to you

Feelings: *'An emotional state or reaction'*[5].

The word that resonates most from the meaning is 'Reaction', which is something done, felt, or thought in response to a situation or event. Do not always believe your feelings because they will lie to you. I've had moments where I feel like everything is going wrong one day and less than twenty-four hours later, I'm skipping around the house feeling amazing again. I cannot, I must not put my trust in how I feel, because my feelings will always change, depending on what I'm dealing with in the moment. My trust must always be in facts.

If Chris and I have a disagreement, sometimes ten minutes later he is fine and wants to have kisses and cuddles, while I'm still re-living the previous hour. Sometimes it takes a minute for my emotions to settle and the truth is, I'm a woman, so this is perfectly normal. But I'm always amazed at how I can feel so annoyed and question whether we will make it, but once I calm down and my feelings change, I

---

[5] https://www.lexico.com/definition/feeling accessed 7th October 2021

feel so in love again. Here we have another example of how feelings flutter and change like butterflies.

Is there anything in your life right now that is frustrating you? Maybe you feel over-worked, tired and like your emotional cup is full. If that's the case, then your decision-making will be cloudy and you shouldn't make any major life decisions based on them. No matter what the situation may be, focus on the truth and take your next step from that place. Take some time to assess things to ensure you're making the correct choices. Nothing is more important than peace of mind, so do whatever is necessary and needed in the moment. Talking to God and externally processing my thoughts always helps me to get my mind in a healthy place. Be easy on yourself because sometimes we can't articulate how we feel or what's happening in our head and that's okay, but eventually you will.

'Life oh life can be beautiful when you take things day by day, life oh life it can pass you by if you let it slip away'
Song: Life
Perspective EP

23

What do you have in your hand?

What do you have in your hand?

I've been writing songs since I was around seven years old. I used to force my sister to listen to all of them and I must be honest, some of them weren't worth her time, but she would always listen and give me feedback. Singing came very naturally to me, but writing didn't and I struggled with English throughout school. It sounds crazy I know, look at me now! I write songs and you're reading my book, life! I found it all really challenging - essays, poetry and writing in general, but I always kept writing and trying. Before I started singing as a solo artiste, I used to sing in a band called *Divine Unity* and I wrote a number of our songs too. So, it's fair to say, writing music has always been part of my life.

In 2017, The Kingdom Choir (the royal wedding choir) began working on some original music. This was well before there were any television cameras or fancy events. We were at a rehearsal and Karen (the founder and leader) asked who would be willing to write some songs. Before I could even volunteer, she pointed to me and said, 'Next week you'll come with a new song.' I could see that even though she asked for volunteers, it was not an option for me and I didn't mind, I was more than happy to write one.

Whilst working one Saturday at my office job, I wrote a song called *Chases*. I quickly recorded it on my phone and I didn't think much about it until it was time to sing it to Karen and the rest of the choir the following week. It was a normal rehearsal in Karen's home and as we sat on her comfy orange sofas, I sang the song. You could hear a pin drop, everyone was silent. When I finished, I was shocked by the response. Everyone loved it and most importantly, Karen liked it and wanted it to be part of our up-coming project.

To cut a very long story short, that song went on to be the only original song included on the Kingdom Choir's debut album, *Stand By Me*. The song was presented to Sony Music who thought it would be a great addition to the album. I mustn't forget to mention, it has been taught all over Europe at gospel workshops and I have received countless messages and videos from people of all ages who have shared their love for the song and what it means to them. There are songs that take weeks, even months for me to complete, but that song took no more than an hour. I call it my God song, because it came straight from Him, for the people who need it. Perfection has never been my goal. As you read above, I always struggled with writing, but I've always used what I have. What about you, what do you have in your hand?

24

friendship

Friendship

At the mature age of thirty-six, I can look back over my life and see where some of my friendships have changed, transitioned and quite frankly, ended. When you're teenager, you can sometimes believe that all your friends will be there, and in some instances, this is the truth. I can remember the feelings I experienced when I realised that some of the people I believed would always be in my close friendship circle, were no longer going to occupy that space in my life, and my goodness, it hurt.

It hurt, because for some of those friendships, you know that things feel differently, but you don't know what you've done to cause this shift and maybe you didn't do anything. I've learnt over the years that it's just not always about you! Everyone sees a situation from their own perspective. In some cases, you grow apart, or maybe jealousy comes in between the friendship. Priorities may change, or maybe the friends just no longer do friendship the way you do. The list could go on forever, but the pain of that transition for me was so hard and I can remember having conversations with my sister and husband, crying, because I didn't like that things were now different.

The good news is that if you've experienced anything like this, the pain eases and eventually for me, disappeared. As time passed, I've worked on my other friendships and I know exactly who my tribe is and who I consider my very close friends. I'm no longer sad about the previous friendships and I'll always share beautiful memories and have history with those people that I'll cherish. However, it's just part of life and it's not always a bad thing. We change, grow, learn and evolve constantly and I truly believe God will give you the people you need around you when you need them most.

Of course, this is not always the case and I can remember my first day of primary school when I met someone who would later become one of my oldest friends. We went through primary and secondary school together and even though through the years we have had our disagreements (which is very normal and healthy), I couldn't get rid of her if I tried and I would not want to. Our lives are different now and for sure busier, but she is one of my best friends for life. She's been so consistent over the years and I would like to think I have done the same for her. When we spend time together, I treasure it and the love we have for each other is real, strong and unbreakable.

Cherish the people who matter to you. If you don't have time to call or see them, as is the case with me sometimes because of my schedule, send a text to let them know you're thinking of them and to check they are okay. We can pretend that we don't need anyone or that our partners, children, jobs etc are all we need, but we're lying to ourselves. We need each other and friendships are to be cherished.

25

You don't need to
change the world just
change your world

You don't need to change the world just change your world

When we think about changing the world it can seem like a massive job that's bigger than we can handle but the truth is, we can all be world changers, we just need to change our world. Mother Teresa said, 'If you want to change the world go home and love your family' and I agree one-hundred per cent.

There's a TV show called *This Is US* and without going into too much detail, it's based around a family of five, Jack and Rebecca who are the parents of triplets Kate, Randall and Kevin. During the series we watch how this family navigate life through the good, the bad, and the ugly. Unfortunately, Jack (the father) passes away rather tragically during the series, but because of it, we witness the remaining family members (especially his three children) trying to face lives' challenges without him.

When Jack passes away his children were seventeen years old, but the impact he had on the family for such a short period of time is phenomenal. From the outside looking in, there's nothing particularly unusual or extremely unique about Jack. He was not famous or rich. He didn't have a special talent and he didn't spend his life in the spotlight, but what he did was to change his world and make a massive impact on the people who were in it. So much so that when his children became adults, they would constantly wonder what advice he would give them in almost every circumstance they faced. Even though he was no longer present in person, his impact and legacy still lived on through his children and his children's children.

Raising a family with all your soul is an amazing thing, but it's not the only way to change your world. Navigating your work life with integrity and kindness and putting someone else's needs before your own are also great. Choosing to smile at the person opposite on the train when you could frown, also works. Helping the poor and giving to charities are all great ways to make an impact in your world. I could go on with a list of different ways to make an impact, because the opportunities are endless. You don't need to be on a stage to reach people, all you have to do is look at how you can help the people in your world. Maya Angelou said, 'I've learned that people will forget what you said, people will forget what you did, but people will never forget how you made them feel.' Don't you dare see yourself or what you bring as small; what's small to you can be huge to the person who needs it. Sometimes I think we underestimate the power of kindness, but considering all the horrible things that are happening in the world right now, kindness is what we all desperately need. Don't over think it, don't get overwhelmed, just take one small step at a time and you'll be amazed how much of an impact you can make to your world.

26

Embrace being
uncomfortable:
that is where you
flourish

Embrace being uncomfortable: that is where you flourish

A little after I got married in 2013, I began travelling and working abroad, leading gospel choir workshops in Europe with the 'God Mother' of UK gospel, Karen Gibson MBE. It's a time of my life that I will always treasure, because I got to experience so many different cultures, amazing food and met some very special people. From the outside, one could assume that all we did was teach people how to sing gospel music, but it was so much more than that. Sometimes the workshops felt like counselling sessions. I used to watch in amazement at how Karen would work so hard, teaching for hours, but also spread love and dispel fear at the same time. It became very normal for me to see people in floods of 'happy' tears throughout the weekend and it was beautiful to witness.

I've never wanted to be a choir conductor and at times I used to ask myself, 'Why am I here? This is not what I want to do'. At the time, I was working as a receptionist, whilst working on my music and going on acting auditions; I knew the experience would be good for me. However, deep down I didn't think I was good at it, I found it so hard and would often try to hide from the responsibility of it, which was impossible, because I would always have to be right in front of the choirs in order to teach. When I began conducting, I was terrified and I would compare myself to Karen constantly, which was my first mistake. She has been conducting and teaching choirs for over twenty years, you just can't beat that length of experience. I also used to struggle to remember all the different harmonies Karen needed me to demonstrate and when you're in front of a choir whose first language is not English and they are depending on you to be sure of what you're doing, it's quite embarrassing when you don't. Karen had no time for my fear and would very often give me a stern but loving talk before, during and after the sessions. She would explain to me that she didn't bring me to know all the harmonies perfectly, but that I should try to be myself, have fun and find a way to spread my joy with the choir. I would try to do this, but when your heart is beating so fast and you're struggling to manage your nerves, it's hard to remember in the moment.

After working with her for around two to three years, we were at a massive festival in Norway, called *Sangfeston*. During a workshop, once again, I didn't quite get the harmony correct. Karen stopped the workshop, sang it to me and waited for me to get it. I would be lying if I said my anxiety didn't kick in, because it did, but for some reason during this session, we connected in a way we hadn't before. I didn't feel like she was pressuring me but rather giving me an invitation to teach in a way that felt totally like me. I also gave myself permission to not be perfect and from that day on I started to enjoy teaching with her so much more than ever before and I began to flourish. My memory improved in regards to remembering harmonies and she would ask me to do warm-ups before and during the sessions, which I loved. I could tell from the response of the people that I had grown, because they trusted me and felt safe. I had accepted that I didn't need to be Karen. I was now relaxed, silly, fun Sharlene, throwing in a dance move or two at any opportunity. From time to time, I still forgot the harmonies, but when that happened, Karen would just correct me and we would move on with the session. She was the expert in the room and I didn't need to try to be her.

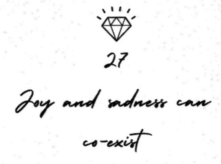

27

Joy and sadness can co-exist

Joy and sadness can co-exist

I am amazed at how Tahlia has only been on this earth for such a short amount of time and she has already made a huge impact in her world. She brings life, light and releases so much joy to those around her every single day.

When I was pregnant with her due the grief I was feeling at the time, It felt like two pieces of my heart had been ripped out and there was no surgery available to repair it. I can remember wondering if she would feel the sadness I was feeling while I was pregnant and if it would somehow impact her, but I'm so happy to announce that did not happen.

I am astonished at how what felt like the worst year of my life can also be the best year of my life all at the same time. Life is a strange and wonderful thing.....! My husband and I were ready to start a family and yes, this felt like the right time but GOD knew when Tahlia needed to make her entrance into this world and His timing is always perfect.

I cried more tears in 2020 than I have ever cried in my whole life. All that being said, I also laughed more than ever before and the memories I have of my loved ones are immeasurable. I say all this to say that joy and sadness can co-exist. Tears of sadness and big belly laughs with tears of joy can happen within the same moments. People are to be cherished and enjoyed.

So, Tahlia Monique Heather Morris, Mummy, Daddy and your entire family just love and adore you and we didn't realise how much we needed you, but we are so happy you're here. Keep being a little world changer baby girl, because I know God's got big plans for you and I am so excited to watch you make your mark on this earth.

'There's always gonna be problems, but I don't focus energy on them. There's always gonna be good things too, it's a reality for me to choose'
Song: Life
Perspective EP

28

Conflict

Conflict

I can remember talking to a couple about marriage once, and one of them proudly shared that they didn't understand how some people say marriage is hard and challenging because they didn't feel that way. For them, marriage had been so easy. At the time, I had only been married for around a year and I thought, *Wow that's amazing! I hope Chris and I can have a marriage like that.* Having being married for eight years, I have come to realise that for that couple, that was beautiful for them, but not realistic for us.

When I look back over my marriage, I can see where we've had small and big conflicts and when those big ones come up, we've had some tough conversations and got to the root of the issue. Our marriage has gone to another level every time those moments have come up. I do struggle to understand how you can have a marriage without any conflict because you're two completely different people with different opinions and Chris and I are not afraid or intimidated to share how we feel, even if the truth hurts the other person's feelings or emotions in that moment.

Lying or pretending that something is okay serves no one and hinders the growth of your marriage or relationship.

Marriage counselling has been a valuable tool for us and helped us work though some of the challenges we've faced as a couple. We had counselling before marriage and I feel extremely blessed to say that the man who counselled us also married us and continues to counsel us during marriage. He has seen our journey from the very beginning, he never takes sides but has an amazing way of getting us unstuck when we feel like we don't understand each other's perspective. Around two years ago, Chris and I had opposite views on something I considered to be very big. I also struggled to see things from his point of view and whenever we tried to discuss it, very often it ended in an argument.

We decided to see our counsellor in an attempt to understand each other. As always, he heard our issue and shared a great story, to try to move us forward. He asked us to imagine we were on our way to France in a boat. He asked Chris if I was on the journey with him, Chris said 'yes.' He then asked Chris if he thought I was in the same boat with him or maybe in a boat next to him, but still journeying to France. Chris indicated that maybe I was in the boat next to him and our counsellor advised that as long as we were still going to the same destination together, it didn't matter that we were not in the same boat; we could still stay connected. Of course, there was more to the session, but that analogy really stayed with me and helped us.

If you're married and feel like your relationship is the only one with challenges, you're not alone. When I think of my marriage with Chris, my overall memories are the great ones. He is my best friend, biggest supporter and the only man I've ever loved. I couldn't imagine doing life without him and I affirm that the challenging moments have served us well and helped to make us both better individually and together as a couple.

In my opinion, conflict in marriage can be a good thing.....

*'Uncomfortable frustrated and exposed, this part of love's reality
is something like a mystery''
Song: Seeing Love
Destiny EP*

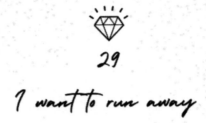

29

I want to run away

I want to run away

Just before Tahlia's first birthday, I was feeling drained and overwhelmed. The lack of sleep, realities of motherhood and my personal work commitments left me feeling like I wanted to run away on a number of occasions. According to BetterHelp, *'People who want to run away are usually stressed or otherwise discontent with their situation and desperately seeking a way out. It could be that you've had enough of the people around you or that the everyday stresses of life have piled up and become overwhelming*[6].

I asked myself what was causing this feeling, because I didn't want to run away from my daughter; I love being her mummy. But I think it was the constant feeling of having to be present and being in desperate need of a break. When I was four months pregnant, we entered a global pandemic, COVID 19, which resulted in a UK lockdown. Life as I knew it was already different because I was housing a baby and then when she was born, caring for a baby, which was a major life adjustment. Being in the house for months, not seeing friends or having physical

---

[6] https://www.betterhelp.com/advice/general/how-to-stop-feeling-like-i-just-want-to-run-away/ accessed 7th October 2021

contact with the people I love, had a huge impact on me. Chris and I were also trying to find our rhythm with work and parenting. I had accepted that balance was no longer the goal and began to wonder what that word meant, because nothing in my current situation felt balanced, but carving out our rhythm felt more realistic.

Even though I was not craving my life before Tahlia, it was the little things that I missed, like eating a meal uninterrupted, washing my hair whilst watching a film, or simply reading a book. I was desperate to find a solution and my sister advised me to take a break and maybe get away with Chris, if possible, but at the time, due to both our individual commitments, it was not. I had to remind myself that this was indeed just a moment. My daughter was only one-year old and of course she needed me. I've had to accept that there will come a point when she doesn't need me quite as much, but while she does, it's important that I embrace it, otherwise I run the risk of missing all the amazing, beautiful things within my current moment.

Sometimes you just have to ride it out and remind yourself that nothing ever stays the same, your moment will eventually change and transition. Running away from something is never the answer, but if you're feeling weary and a break is not possible, take a deep breath in and out, make time for laughter (if you can), do some physical exercise and take things one week, one day and sometimes one hour at a time. Praying and meditating on God always helps to get my mind at peace and in the right place. If you're a parent like me, remember that the days are long, but the years are short. You'll never get these precious moments back.....

Galatians 6:9 (NKJV)
'And let us not grow weary while doing good, for in due season we shall reap if we do not lose heart'

30

God always speaks to
me

God always speaks to me

The best thing about hearing God speak, is the experience felt when He does. Out of all the things I desire in life, peace of mind is at the top of my list. I always think of my life like a puzzle; whereby my problems are one piece and oftentimes that's all I can see. But God sees the whole puzzle and the whole picture. He knows exactly how your current moment fits into a bigger plan, so when He gives direction, I always listen.

Growing in my faith and building a relationship with God has been a beautiful journey, even when it's felt challenging. His voice sounds like my voice. His voice provides reason in a situation. I often refer to His voice as a traffic light system. When faced with the uncertainty of what to do in a moment, or unsure of a decision I need to make, it's not often I get a green light to say 'go' or 'yes', but deep down, I always know when it's a red light telling me 'no' or to choose a different path. Hearing God's voice is my absolute favourite thing in the world. It's hard to articulate how much it means to me, but it is everything!

Some of my most challenging situations have been more bearable because God has spoken. In my eight years of marriage, I've been so confused about what to do at times and I can list numerous occasions where God will let me know exactly what the problem is. It's not always fun when He reveals that I'm the problem, but none the less, His voice makes all the difference.

There is a verse in the Bible in 1 Peter 5:7 that says, 'Casting all your cares upon Him, for He cares for you' (NKJV). This scripture is saying, tell God everything; the big, the small or even what seems insignificant to you, because He's interested in it all.

When I'm confused, worried or stressed I always speak to God. It's not complicated; praying is simply talking to God and I can do that everywhere and anywhere. The beautiful thing about building a relationship with God is that He speaks back to me and when He does, it changes everything. Speak to Him when you're happy as well as when you're sad. He cares about every detail of your life, so share it all with Him.

I believe God is always speaking, but we're not always aware of the different ways He speaks. We also can be so busy that we need to pause to hear His voice. Wherever you are at on this interesting road we call life, have a chat to Him today. You might just get some long-awaited answers you've been seeking; but you'll most definitely find peace in your pursuit of them.

31

Gratitude and

contentment

Gratitude and contentment

If you scroll through your social media on a Monday morning, I'm pretty sure you'll see a quote that relates to gratitude. I can understand if you feel like its overused, but practicing gratitude has helped me to manage so many of the different stages in my life. It's something I have done for years and when you do it consistently you reap the benefits. I try my best not to focus my attention on the things I don't have, but sometimes I am guilty of it and when I lose focus, I pull out my secret weapon and that's 'thankfulness'. Try to look at what you currently have that was once a dream, that is now your reality, if you need a reminder on perspective. Find gratitude in the big and small.

Learning to be content with little and much has been one of my biggest tools. I have a very long list of things I desire, but staying thankful for them all keeps me peaceful and reminds me to treasure every day. I'm very aware of the reality of death and even though I don't dwell on it, when I find myself complaining about any area of life, I remember that every day I am alive is a gift - embrace it and live with a great sense of contentment. I've never been into nature very much, but during lockdown, I spent many hours outside, staring into nature, taking deep breaths and forcing myself to take in the beauty that I saw. There's beauty all around us. Sometimes you just need to pause and look around you to see it.

Philippians 4:11-13 (NIV)
'I am not saying this because I am in need, for I have learned to be content whatever the circumstances. I know what it is to be in need, and I know what it is to have plenty. I have learned the secret of being content in any and every situation, whether well fed or hungry, whether living in plenty or in want. I can do all this through him who gives me strength.'

'Everything that you lose is not what you choose, gratitude is the key to all that you need'
Song: Life
Perspective EP